Soar!
Beyond the Heels of Adversity

By: Shevelle McPherson, Esq.

Copyright © 2016 by Shevelle McPherson, All rights reserved. No part of this book may be reproduced in any form without the written permission of the author and its publisher.

Table of Contents

Dedication i
Introduction iii
Biography v
Chapter 1: Determination 1
    Physically Challenged 2
    No Pain, No Gain 16
    From Tragedy to Triumph 19
Chapter 2: Drive 29
    Teenage Pregnancy 30
    Pregnancy to Promise 38
Chapter 3: Optimism 51
    Terminated 52
    One Door Closes but a Better Door Opens 61
Chapter 4: Open-Mindedness 67
    Application Denied 68
    From Thinking Small to Dreaming Big 72
Chapter 5: Persistence 79
    Not Accepted 80
    No to Yes 85
Chapter 6: Motivation 93
    The Position Has Been Filled 94

Disappointment to Destiny...................... 106

Chapter 7: Self-Worth & Self-Esteem 111

No Promotion..112

Stagnant to Self-Development..................116

Chapter 8: Faith 123

What's Next? 124

Employed to Self-Employed 129

Chapter 9: Purpose 139

Not Completely Fulfilled.......................... 140

From Merely Existing to Living in Purpose 144

Chapter 10: S.O.A.R. 147

Honing in on the 8 Character Traits that will Propel You to S.O.A.R. 148

Dedication

This book is dedicated to my beloved grandmother, Maude Parker, and my son, Lamar McPherson. These two people have impacted my life so much.

My grandmother was the most selfless person I know. She was a living example of the "giving tree." She gave everything from the heart and never expected anything in return. She seemed to have passed that trait on to me.

She taught me to love, to forgive, and most importantly, to pray. Because of her and the power of prayer, I have been able to soar and come to live in my divine purpose. As a result, I am now able to share my gift with the world—my story.

As for my son Lamar, you changed the path of my life. You appeared under the guise of an adversity, but as it turns out, you were the greatest blessing ever bestowed upon me. You are the reason I pressed through life, driven to soar beyond every impending difficulty.

God entrusted me with your life, so failure was never an option. I dedicated my life to creating opportunities for you, and now, I dedicate this book to you as proof of God's blessing over your life.

Introduction

The purpose of this book is to share my personal experiences that became catalysts for some of my most significant breakthroughs. Through this book, I invite you to walk alongside me as I take you on my journey, revealing some of the adversities I encountered along the way.

These adversities are not uncommon, but I reveal how they led me to recognize and engage eight essential character traits that changed my mindset, propelling me to soar beyond those adversities and land in my divine purpose. We all have these character traits; we just have to identify and ignite them!

I hope my experiences will help you recognize similar situations along your journey through life and empower you to discover and cultivate these same character traits in yourself so you, too, can soar beyond your adversities and live the abundant, purposeful life you are destined to live.

I pray that every person who reads this book will be transformed for the better. I also pray that each of you will embrace the adversities of life, realizing that obstacles are simply opportunities for you to become great!

Biography

I was born in a depressed neighborhood in Newark, New Jersey. My parents were divorced, so my brother Cleveland Jr. (Shahid), and I grew up in a single-parent home with our mother, who worked two jobs to make ends meet. She was consumed with work and left with very little time to parent. My father was often preoccupied with his own survival. I don't recall ever living with my dad as a child, although he has always been present in my life, and we have always maintained a special relationship. To this day, I still call him my "Poppadoppalis."

My brother and I called ourselves "latchkey kids." We kept the key to our apartment tied on a string around our necks. My mother wasn't around often, so we would come and go like little adults. I looked forward to the weekends, summers, and holidays because I got to go to my grandmother's house. I went there every Friday after school and stayed there until Sunday night.

I spent the entire summer and every school break at my grandma's house. I can't express enough how much I loved my grandma. On Saturdays, we would hang out together, go grocery shopping, or run errands or, if it was nice outside, just sit on the porch. It didn't matter what I did with my grandma; I just enjoyed being in her company.

On Sundays, we went to church, Abyssinian Baptist Church on West Kinney Street in Newark. My grandmother was a very spiritual woman.

She kept her Bible open on the night stand next to her bed and loved going to church, so I learned to love it, too. I even sang in the junior choir. I often accompanied my grandma to her church group meetings.

She only had an 8th grade education, but she knew how to read her Bible, and she read it every single night. I was not allowed to go to bed until I dropped to my knees and said my bedtime prayers. We said our prayers together every night. We prayed so often that I believe she left a permanent blessing on my life. Praying every night and every morning became a ritual. It's one of the best habits I developed. I continue to practice that habit to this very day.

I attended Warren Street School in

Newark for first and second grade. I remember my first day at that public school like it was yesterday. I remember being so shy that I wet myself because I was too afraid to raise my hand to ask to go to the bathroom. However, I don't remember much else about that school.

I vaguely recall walking to and from school with my brother. It was a rough neighborhood, and we often saw fights after school and lots of bullying.

I also remember my second grade teacher, Mrs. Clark. She was a member of Abyssinian Baptist church too. She was nice and was an excellent teacher, but Warren Street School was an inner city school plagued with inner city problems. I'm certain that made her job challenging.

My mother wasn't the perfect

mother, but she tried her darnest to be. She wasn't very emotional and at times seemed quite distant. Despite her shortcomings, she loved her children dearly.

The best thing my mother ever gave me was the opportunity to get a good education, despite the financial challenge. She saw something special in me at a young age. I was inquisitive and always showed an interest in learning. As a result, my mother wanted me to get the best education possible. After second grade, my mother enrolled me in private school. It was a huge sacrifice, but I believe the education I received in my early childhood greatly contributed to my continued success in school.

In third grade I began attending

Queen of Angels School in Newark. This was the beginning of the journey to my destiny. Ironically, it is also when I began to face many obstacles. Interestingly, those very same obstacles have all shaped my life and have ultimately led me to become the strong woman that I am today.

My awesome third grade teacher was Ms. Paglioni. The learning environment at Queen of Angels School was much better than my old school. This was my first encounter with the old adage "You get what you pay for." I loved this school. I made good friends, had excellent teachers, and began thriving there. Then on January 9, 1980, all of that changed. I faced my first tragedy. My life changed in an instant. Little did I know, my journey to destiny was about to begin . . .

Chapter 1: Determination

Have you ever felt like giving up? Hopeless? Or that a situation was just too hard to overcome and that it would be easier to just accept things for what they were? To accept your situation as your fate in life?

*If you answered "yes" to any of these questions, it is time to identify and ignite your **"determination"** character trait!*

Physically Challenged

"You May Never Walk Again"

On January 9, 1980, a cold winter afternoon, school had just let out. I crossed the street to catch the bus home. As I was standing at the bus stop waiting on my bus to arrive, I looked back across the street and saw a group of my friends playing joyfully in front of the school. Eager to join in the fun, I decided to go back to play with them until my bus arrived.

I looked down the street and didn't see my bus anywhere. As I crossed the street, a car suddenly appeared. The drunk driver behind the wheel struck me with his car so hard that I was flung high into the air. My body went into shock, but

I recall striking my head on a parked car and my body smashing into the pavement as I landed in the middle of the street.

Afterward, I lay there with my head bleeding profusely and my legs twisted up like a pretzel. I was disoriented and, obviously, unable to walk.

I could hear people screaming "don't move" but all I could think about was another car not seeing my small twisted body lying in the middle of the road and then striking me again.

It was at that moment that I became empowered with what I can only describe as an angelic power. I was somehow able to muster enough strength to scoot out of the middle of the street and onto the side of the road until an ambulance arrived.

I recall my cousin Fleming Jr., my mom, my cousin Fran, and my brother Shahid arriving at the scene of the accident before the ambulance arrived to transport me to the hospital. I still remember the looks of shock and despair on their faces as they stared speechless at my twisted, feeble body lying practically lifeless in the street.

The ambulance driver faced the challenge of rushing me to the hospital, while causing me the least amount of pain possible, but those two tasks could not be simultaneously accomplished. Every pothole and crack in the pavement caused the ambulance to jolt, which made me scream in excruciating pain. The slightest movement caused my legs to rattle. It literally felt like every bone in my body was loose and shattered. When we arrived at the hospital, the medical staff was waiting, prepared to begin treating me immediately.

The doctors determined that I had suffered a concussion along with a deep gash in my forehead, a severely fractured right leg, and a broken left leg. After my initial examination, my forehead was sutured, my legs were temporarily stabilized, and I was prepped for emergency surgery. My father had arrived shortly after the ambulance did, and he keenly observed every medical procedure performed on me.

Early the following morning, January 10, I was taken to surgery, which lasted several hours. After the surgery, the lead physician spoke with my family about my condition. He reported that my broken left leg was set. My right leg was fractured in so many places, including my growth plate, that it resembled a jigsaw puzzle. He struggled to repair it. He had to insert temporary pins in my knee area, so that procedure would require a follow up surgery. He mentioned some permanent damage to my right leg, but overall, he considered the operation to be successful.

I anticipated a long road to recovery.

After that first surgery, I wore a body cast. It covered both legs and went all the way up past my waist, stopping at my chest so my arms were still free. I was bedridden, and getting up to go to the bathroom was not an option. I was restricted to using a bed pan.

I recall the doctors visiting my

hospital room every day after that first surgery and sticking a pin in my toe, asking, "Can you feel this?" Each day I would reply, "No." This practice went on daily for weeks.

Although no one said anything directly to me, even at the tender age of 9, I assumed that if I didn't begin to feel something in my toe, I would end up paralyzed and unable to walk again. I thought that no one wanted to tell me, though, because they hoped that my condition would improve.

I often saw the doctors looking concerned as they huddled for discussion after each examination. They would then pull my parents aside to privately discuss my medical condition. I couldn't hear those conversations, but I could sense what they were saying. It was not good.

As if all the whispering and not having any feeling in my toe wasn't concerning enough, I subsequently learned more about the permanent damage in my right leg. The doctor finally explained it to me. He said, "Your right leg was fractured in the growth plate. As a result, your right leg will stop growing soon. We will continue monitoring it, but until it stops growing, there is nothing else we can do."

That meant that, even if I were somehow able to regain feeling in my right toe and leg and were able to walk again, I would still be handicapped. The damage to my right leg's growth plate would cause my right leg to cease growing soon, but my left leg would continue to grow. I would ultimately have to wear a special orthopedic shoe to equalize the disparity in the length of my legs.

This was devastating news to a third grader. I hadn't even made it to high school yet. So many thoughts were racing through my head: Would I ever be able to be a cheerleader or play soccer, basketball, or any sport for that matter? My future seemed so bleak.

I prepared myself for a long healing process.

On January 25, I was released from the hospital, still in a body cast, so a hospital bed was delivered to my house because I needed the trapeze component to help lift myself up and down to use the bed pan. I would need around-the-clock care, so my mother took a leave-ofabsence from her job and began to take care of me at home.

On February 14, I was admitted back into the hospital for a second surgery to remove the pins that were inserted in my right knee during the first surgery. I remained in the hospital until February 22. My mom had been unable to work since my car accident and never left my bedside, but it was becoming financially difficult for her to continue caring for me. She still needed to keep a roof over our heads and provide for herself and my brother, despite my medical situation.

That was when my grandmother stepped in. She told my mom to return to work full-time and let me stay with her once I was released from the hospital. She agreed to take over caring for me. I love my mom to pieces, but my grandma held a special place in my heart too, so I knew I wouldn't mind staying with her as I recovered. I actually began to look forward to being discharged from the hospital and going to my grandma's house. After my hospital release, I moved in with my grandma for the remainder of my recovery.

I was no longer in a body cast when I was discharged from the hospital this time. However, each of my legs was in a separate cast, so I was still unable to walk and return to school. As a result, I was assigned a private tutor so I could be home schooled. My tutor came to my grandmother's house every day so I could keep up with my lessons. I made a special request that he not come when *Guiding Light* was on because that was my grandma's favorite soap opera, and I watched it with her religiously. We didn't want to be disturbed during our show.

Caring for me was a challenge for my grandmother. I didn't have a hospital bed at her house, so my grandma had to lift me frequently throughout the day. I could tell that my caretaking was taking a toll on her health, but she never said a word. My grandmother was not one to complain; she was the "giving tree," after all. She was dedicated to caring for me no matter what. She ended up in the hospital several months later, though, because she had developed a hernia as a result of constantly lifting me.

On March 28, one of my casts was removed. This time, when the doctor stuck a pin in my toe and asked the infamous question, "Can you feel this?" I yelled, "Ouch!" That was the greatest pain I ever felt. Ahhh . . . It hurt so good! That was the first time I had feeling in my toe since the accident. To me, that pain signified that I would walk again: I was not going to be paralyzed. *To God be the Glory!* Shortly thereafter, my other cast was removed. It was now time to start walking. I was so excited but didn't realize the road to recovery was far from over.

After having both legs in a cast and lying on my back for several months, I needed physical therapy. When my doctor told me that I was ready to begin, I was so excited. I began to look forward to physical therapy because I was so anxious to walk again.

To my surprise, physical therapy

was a challenge. I didn't realize how painful and grueling this journey was going to be. I literally had to learn how to walk all over again.

I recall the first day of physical therapy when I simply put my feet down on the floor and tried to stand up for the first time in months. At that moment, I felt the most excruciating pain I have ever felt in my entire life. I sat right back down and didn't want to ever stand back up again. My physical therapist explained to me that the pain I felt was from the simple flow of blood traveling to my lower limbs. Because I had been bedridden for several months prior, blood hadn't been circulating to my lower extremities as it once did.

We take so many things in life for

granted, such as breathing, sitting, standing, brushing our teeth—tasks we don't even think about when we perform them because they are routine. It is not until you actually experience a tragedy that leaves you unable to stand, walk, or do other basic daily tasks that you realize how blessed you were to have been able to perform those ordinary tasks.

My parents were distraught during this entire ordeal. My mother would leave work, excited to come to my physical therapy sessions, only to watch in disappointment as I refused to even try. She tried her best to cheer me on and encourage me, but to no avail. At that point, her dream was not for me to be a doctor, lawyer, or even a cheerleader. Her dream was to just see me walk again. I was 9 years old, and I had already experienced so much pain that I was ready to give up. I did not want to endure physical therapy. I thought I would accept being wheelchair-bound because the pain of standing was just too excruciating. I was able to sleep through my painful surgeries, but physical therapy was a lot different.

No Pain, No Gain

Every time they wheeled me in to physical therapy, I would cry. It broke my mother's heart to watch me go through so much agony. No mother wants to see her child suffer like I was suffering. It finally became too much for her to bear, so she stopped coming to my physical therapy sessions.

One day as I sat in my wheelchair at physical therapy feeling hopeless and steadfast on giving up, my physical therapist asked, "Are you going to come here every day and just sit there?" I replied, "Yup."

She began to remind me of all that I had already endured and overcome. She also reminded me of what my mother and grandmother had endured in taking care of me. She said, "Your grandmother suffered a hernia from lifting you several times a day and didn't let that stop her. Your mother nearly lost her job sitting by your bed side day and night, refusing to leave until your grandmother assured her she would take over caring for you." She continued, "Your father tries to appear strong, but we all know he is hurting inside. And your friends must miss running around and playing with you." She continued to speak life into me. She finally said, "It is time for you to get up out of that wheelchair and try really hard to push past the pain. I promise you that the pain won't last forever."

My physical therapist had become my first life coach. At that moment, something inside of me clicked. My physical therapist was right: my mother and grandmother sacrificed a lot while caring for me. I didn't want to disappoint them or be a burden on them for the rest of my life. I also thought about my life before the accident. I really missed walking and running around with my friends. I realized that I had to get out of that wheelchair, not only for me, but for the people who I loved and who loved me. I identified and ignited my determination character trait! My determination set in, and I decided to do whatever it took to walk again.

From Tragedy to Triumph

It was time to stand up and face the pain head on.

The first few physical therapy sessions were so painful that all I could do was stand. Determined to prevail, I did what I could—some days I would just stand. I would let the blood painfully circulate through my limbs. I endured the aching over and over again until my body finally got used to the flow of blood traveling to my lower extremities once again. Eventually, I was able to take a few steps holding onto the railings. After weeks of continuing to endure physical therapy, I was able to take a few steps, unassisted. It wasn't easy, but I found out it was possible. I became determined to make a full recovery and walk, especially for my mother and grandmother.

I noticed that, each day, the pain subsided little by little until finally, after weeks of grueling physical therapy, I learned to walk again. On May 11, I gave my mom the best Mother's Day gift ever. I surprised her by walking for her. The look on her face was priceless. It was a look that I will never forget.

I wasn't ready to run a marathon, but I was able to walk a short distance unassisted. I was making great progress. I was putting forth the effort, and I was overcoming my physical challenges. I ultimately made a full recovery and began to walk unassisted, without pain.

When I returned to school in the fourth grade, my doctors continued to monitor my right leg. Two years after the accident, my doctors discovered that my right leg had stopped growing as previously predicted. My mom consulted an orthopedic specialist to discuss all available options and included me in the decision-making process. After all, they were my legs.

We were told that nothing could be done for the right leg. However, I had two options to consider with respect to my left leg. 1) I could let my left leg continue to outgrow the right leg and end up with one leg much longer than the other, leading me to wear a special orthopedic shoe on my right leg for the rest of my life. The orthopedic shoe would even out the disparity in the length of my legs. Or 2) I could have my orthopedic surgeon, Dr. McKeon, perform a special type of corrective surgery on my left leg. The procedure would involve inhibiting the growth plate so my left leg would stop growing, as well. That would prevent me from having a disparity in my leg lengths. It also meant that I wouldn't have to wear a special orthopedic shoe for the rest of my life. I would someday be able to actually wear high heels. That decision became a no-brainer for the little fashionista buried inside of me. I eagerly elected the latter option.

On March 29, 1982, I had my final surgery. I had already discovered my determination trait, so it was time to re-ignite it.

I accepted the challenges on the road to recovery, this time around with little squabble. After the surgery, I once again endured physical therapy. It wasn't as bad the second time. I was ultimately walking again with two efficient—and pretty much even—legs. I did not end up paralyzed, or disabled. Today, I stand 5'6" and proudly walk in my high heels with the strength and courage of a lion.

I could have let this tragic experience ruin me, and until I ignited my determination trait, it almost did. I could have given up and refused to endure the painful physical therapy. I could have succumbed to depression and sulked in self-pity. I could have chosen to be permanently disabled, electing not to have the corrective surgery and just accept my looming fate. But I decided not to accept that outcome. I became determined!

I decided at just 9 years old that I

would be brave. I would fight hard and put in the work at physical therapy to regain my health and ultimately walk again. I made the bold decision at 11 years old to have my growth stunted in my left leg rather than becoming disabled for the rest of my life. I decided not to let the pain stop me from pushing forward. Yes, my determination was initially tested, but once it was ignited, I faced my adversity head on. Through the process, I learned to endure, to be strong, and to be brave, and that pain doesn't last forever. I also learned that, with determination, I can overcome anything, no matter what!

Ignite Your Power

When a tragedy appears in your life, whether it is a car accident, a medical diagnosis, or other life-altering or apparently devastating event, focus on someone or something in your life that is worth fighting for to help you ignite your determination character trait and overcome that tragedy. Remember how I thought about my grandmother and mother as I sat in that wheelchair ready to give up? Some people in your life will stand by your side no matter what. Those same people are worth your determination, so fight and survive for them.

If you think you don't have something or someone, look in the mirror. Do it for you. You are worth fighting for. You were destined to be here, so don't bow out easily. I wanted to conquer my tragedy, not just for my family, but for me; I wanted to resume the life I had before my accident.

Don't get discouraged if you can't conquer a tragedy quickly. Just become determined to conquer it.

Sometimes you have to be determined to start wherever you are in the process. Starting with small goals can make a long process seem manageable. For a time, all I could do was stand, so I just stood. But with hard work and determination, I persevered to do more than just stand, I took a few steps, and then, I eventually walked again. What began as a tragedy for me ended up a triumph because I became determined. I am living proof that no accident or tragedy can destroy you or cause you to give up unless you succumb to your circumstances.

A lesson hides in every tragic situation. For me, I needed to learn to identify, strengthen and ignite my determination trait so I could endure the pain and suffering necessary to ultimately experience the joy and pleasure of walking again. You may have to experience the pain of a tragedy to get to the joy of the triumph, so don't let a tragedy or tragic news halt your journey in life. Instead, let it toughen you up and strengthen you.

Be determined to prevail against whatever odds you are facing. Remember, with determination, we all have the power to turn our tragedies into triumphs. So, when tragedy strikes, get determined, and soar!

Chapter 2: Drive

> *Have you ever lacked ambition? Felt unmotivated to strive for more? Felt trapped in a situation that caused you to settle? Or were/are you surrounded by apathetic people who have caused you, whether consciously or subconsciously, to be lazy too? If you answered "yes" to any of those questions, you need to identify and ignite your "**drive**" character trait!*

Teenage Pregnancy

"You are Going to be a Teenage Mother"

When I was in the 10th grade, attending Essex Catholic High School in Irvington, NJ, no one was surprised that I was an honor student because I had always excelled at school. I had many friends at my school, but I was also a teenager starting to venture out into my urban neighborhood, developing friendships with other teenagers there, as well.

Sometimes, it seemed like I was living two separate lives with two separate groups of friends.

I still lived in Newark with my

mother, brother Cleveland Jr. (Shahid), and now my younger sister Shakeerah, too. Every day, I would catch a bus out of the inner city to my Catholic high school. Monday through Friday, I was a dedicated student, laser-focused on my school work. On weekends and on school breaks, though, I would hang out with my neighborhood friends in Newark. Soon, I started dating a young man from my neighborhood, and after about a year, I received what, at the time, was devastating news. I was pregnant!

I recall my mother and father sitting me down and saying, "You are a child, but you are now living with an adult situation and will be taking on adult responsibilities." This was one of the most difficult moments of my life. I was 15 years old and pregnant. My mind began to race. Statistically, I was doomed.

According to statistics, I would have more children out of wedlock before the age of 18, I would become a high school dropout, and I would end up living off of public assistance for the rest of my life. I was terrified.

Then on April 26, of my sophomore year of high school, I gave birth to my son Lamar Marquis McPherson. He was born two months premature. My parental role had begun.

Initially, Lamar's father stepped up to the plate and assumed his responsibility as father. He was 17 years old and accepted his new parental responsibilities without hesitation. He began working a full-time job and was responsible for financially providing for both Lamar and me. I continued to attend my Catholic high school and continued to excel.

Fortunately, I lived rent free at home with my mother, and with the financial assistance from Lamar's father, I didn't have much of a financial struggle. However, time-wise, parenting was draining me. I had to catch a bus to my grandmother's house in the morning to drop Lamar off so she could babysit him while I attended school. From there, I would catch a bus to my high school. After school, I rode a bus back to my grandmother's house to pick Lamar up. We would then ride a bus back home where I would complete schoolwork and then continue caring for Lamar.

The additional travel time was

exhausting, let alone the late nights and broken sleep from caring for a newborn. It was challenging trying to function while so sleep deprived. I often went to school extremely tired.

One day at school, my teacher had to tap me on the shoulder because I slept through the bell ringing for us to change classes. All the students, except me, had left the classroom. I remained in my seat, dead asleep at my desk.

Another time, I woke up in the middle of the night to feed Lamar, but I fell asleep again while the bottle was still on the stove warming. I recall jumping up to the sound of the fire alarm, seeing nothing but smoke. I was home alone with my son and little sister, and I dragged them both out of the house through a fog of smoke, unable to see anything. I refused to wait on the fire department, fearing we would all be dead by the time they arrived. I nearly set the entire apartment on fire.

After that dangerous incident, my grandmother again took action. She knew it was overwhelming for me to care for an infant and finish high school at the same time, so she insisted that I let my son stay with her Monday through Friday and then pick him up Friday after school and keep him until Sunday night. She wanted me to focus on completing the last two months of the school year. I knew she was right, so I accepted her offer.

When summer arrived, I was able to care for Lamar more. With my grandma's assistance, I was also able to work a summer job through a teen summer work program. Over the summer, Lamar and I practically lived at my grandma's house.

All seemed to be going well. Lamar's father continued to be financially supportive by working full-time to provide for his son. However, that soon changed.

Lamar's fathers' usual walk to work was through the neighborhood. As he passed the gangbangers and drug dealers every day on his way to work, he was constantly pressured to quit his job and join the "street hustle." The dealers told him he could make more in a day on the street than he made in a week at his job.

He often told me about these daily encounters, but I didn't learn until it was too late that he finally accepted an offer to become a neighborhood drug dealer. He was ultimately arrested and sent to jail for 3 years, leaving me to raise my son alone.

At 16 years old, I was truly a single parent. I continued attending high school and was doing well academically, but I didn't have any genuine future goals. I had one agenda: graduate high school, get a job, and move out of my mother's apartment. In my neighborhood, the general consensus was that you graduate high school, if you are lucky, and then you get a job and move out. Period.

My parents were not college graduates—they both had GEDs. Although my parents had a strong work ethic, they had no higher education and, thus, did not encourage me to continue my education past high school. Higher education was never a topic of conversation in my house. I know my parents wanted the best for me and my siblings, but I honestly don't know if they understood what "the best" was.

I was surrounded by a neighborhood of family and friends who weren't goal oriented. Drive and ambition just didn't exist in my family or my neighborhood. I, therefore, developed the same lackadaisical attitude.

I knew I wanted the best for Lamar, but I didn't have any long-term goals. However, that soon changed.

<u>Pregnancy to Promise</u>

I wanted Lamar to have the best life possible, but like my parents, I don't think I knew how to give him that "best life." Then one day during my senior year in high school, I was called to my guidance counselor Ms. Gideon's office. I was a teenage mother with a lot of responsibilities, but I attended all my classes and submitted all my assignments on time. I was also a member of the National Honor Society and an honor roll student, so I was baffled as to why I was being summoned to see her.

Once I arrived, Ms. Gideon invited me in and asked me to close the door and have a seat. She then pulled out a file, put on her glasses, and began flipping through the pages. When she finished, she removed her glasses, set the folder down, and looked up at me with great concern. Finally, she asked, "Have you applied to any colleges?"

I thought to myself, "College? I'm

not going to college." I quickly responded, "No." She then replied, "You are a senior and will be graduating soon. What do you plan to do with your life?" I responded, "I am going to get a job, move out of my mother's apartment, and take care of my son."

She then engaged me in a conversation that would change my entire mindset and life from that day forward. Unbeknownst to me at the time, Ms. Gideon had just become my second life coach.

She told me how important it was that I obtain higher education and said, "You *need* to apply to college." I had never even thought about going. I replied, "I am a teenage mother, and I do not have the option of going away to college like my classmates. I refuse to leave Lamar for four years to be raised by family members."

I didn't understand why we were even having this conversation.

I recalled hearing about many of my classmates applying to colleges and visiting different college campuses with their parents. They were returning to school, sharing stories about which schools they liked. They would come to class excited when they received their various acceptance letters.

I, on the other hand, attended class daily and went home to complete my school assignments and take care of my son. My family never discussed college or my future. Ms. Gideon was the first person to bring up the possibility of me attending college.

Ms. Gideon was adamant. She introduced me to the possibility of pursing post-secondary education. She said: "You don't have to go away to attend college. You live 15 minutes away from Rutgers University and 30 minutes away from both Kean University and Montclair State—all schools you can commute to." She insisted that I apply to a few local colleges. I replied, "I can't afford the application fees, let alone the college tuition. I don't have some magical college trust fund set aside for me somewhere." She said, "I will help you get the application fees waived, and I will also help you apply for financial aid." She was relentless. She showed me statistics for jobs and salaries comparing people with just a high school diploma and those with a college degree. I was shocked. Ms. Gideon had just convinced me to apply to college. I finally replied, "I will apply."

For the first time in my life, I was seriously thinking about my future. I began to understand the excitement my classmates felt when they came back from visiting Morgan State, Hampton University, Howard University, and all the other schools they conversed about. Realizing you have the power to drastically change your destiny and live more than a mediocre life is exciting. I knew I wanted Lamar to have a better life, but until that day, I had no idea how I was going to offer him one.

Ms. Gideon provided me with a roadmap! Guidance!

Visiting her office became a daily

ritual. She reviewed my applications and essays and helped me apply to several colleges. She opened my eyes to future possibilities and showed me the blueprint I needed to give Lamar a better life.

First, she made me recognize that I had to start by giving *myself* a chance at a better life. I had to educate and empower myself so I would be positioned to do the same for my son. I had to be the catalyst for change in my family. I realized that I wanted to be a role model for Lamar and my younger sister Shakeerah because I didn't have any role models who I could pick up the phone and call when I was growing up. I wanted to position myself to be that for both my son and my sister. With Ms. Gideon's help, I had identified and ignited my drive character trait! I became driven.

As it turns out, I was accepted to all the local colleges I applied to, but I was most interested in going to Rutgers University in Newark. Besides being one of the best universities in New Jersey, it was also within walking distance of both my house and the daycare center Lamar would be attending.

After graduating from high school, I began attending Rutgers full time during the day while Lamar attended daycare. Because his father was incarcerated, I took on a full-time job as a security guard at night to provide for Lamar. I managed to get by on periodic naps. Because I was attending college and working full time, I started to engage with more goal-oriented people. My classmates and my co-workers all seemed to have future plans and goals. Many of the other security guards were students, too. Working that job was perfect because we were able to earn a paycheck while having an opportunity to study as we sat at a desk securing a building or guarding a post. Being around these goal-oriented people led me to amp up my drive and my goals.

While I was attending Rutgers, I enrolled in a real estate course, passed a state examination, and became a licensed realtor. I also enrolled in a tax preparation course at H&R Block and worked as a seasonal tax preparer. I eventually opened up a seasonal tax business of my own. I was driven to succeed so that both Lamar and I could have a better life and greater opportunities.

I graduated from Rutgers University's dual degree program with a bachelor's degree in accounting and business management. I was the first person in my family to graduate from college.

During my last year of college, I took a business law class that piqued my interest in law school. Around the same time, my brother Shahid was standing trial in federal court. As I observed some of his trial, I didn't think he had competent legal counsel. I began contemplating attending law school but wasn't quite convinced I could handle the commitment of such a rigorous program while being a single mother. However, now that I had tapped into my drive trait, the desire for higher achievement continued to simmer.

Ignite Your Power

If you encounter a situation that leaves you feeling hopeless or mediocre, it is time to ignite your drive character trait! Igniting your drive will cause a complete shift in your mindset and your behavior. You will notice yourself broadening your horizons and wanting so much more out of life. What I initially thought was an adversity—my teenage pregnancy and the birth of my son Lamar—resulted in me identifying, strengthening, and igniting my drive. I ended up having a beautiful son who drove me to aspire to live an abundant life so I could give him the opportunity to live abundantly, too.

Take a moment to evaluate your goals, your environment, the company you keep, and the limitations you may be imposing upon yourself. It could be time to surround yourself with more goal-oriented people and raise the bar on your drive. Eliminate all the limiting beliefs that you place on yourself or that you allow others to place on you.

You have the ability to push beyond mediocrity. You are pregnant with endless possibilities, and it is time to breathe life into them. Push out the drive that's buried inside of you. Be driven to go forth and soar!

Chapter 3: Optimism

> *Have you ever been discouraged? Felt like everything was going wrong? Received bad news that caused you to feel pessimistic? Felt like a door to an opportunity just closed? If you answered "yes" to any of these questions, you need to identify and ignite your **"optimism"** character trait!*

Terminated

"You Don't Seem to Be Happy Here"

Upon graduating from college, I transferred out of the security department at the corporation where I worked and began working in the accounting department. I continued to contemplate law school for several months, but I always dismissed the thought because of the time and financial commitment I would have to take on in addition to being a single parent. Instead, I decided to enter the paralegal profession, so I enrolled in an American Bar Association–approved paralegal program at Farleigh Dickinson University.

While I was in this program, I decided to pursue an internship, as well, because it would allow me the opportunity to work for an attorney for free in exchange for paralegal experience. I knew that experience would prove beneficial when I finally graduated from the paralegal program and sought permanent employment.

While perusing the paralegal intern position listings at my school's Career Placement Center, I saw a listing for an attorney seeking a bankruptcy paralegal intern. I had moved to South Orange, NJ, and the firm was practically right around the corner from my house. I submitted my resume and was soon called in for an interview.

I recall sitting in the waiting area at

the Law Offices of John Wise, Esq., waiting to be called in for my interview. I was nervous because I felt like this would be the perfect internship opportunity, so I said a prayer.

Soon, I was escorted into Mr. Wise's office. He was a tall, thin man, and as I walked in, he was staring down at what I assumed was my resume. He then looked up at me and asked, "Why are you here?" I thought to myself, "Uh duh. Why is he asking me this? Obviously, I am here to interview for the paralegal intern position that he advertised for." I then responded, "I'm here in response to your paralegal intern listing posted at my school."

He glanced down at my resume once more, looked up, and responded,

"You should be in law school." I was caught off guard and instantly replied, "Excuse me?" He answered, "You appear to be very intelligent, young, African American female, and you should be in law school. The legal profession needs more lawyers like you."

At that moment Mr. Wise became my third life coach. Just moments earlier I was sitting in the lobby, nervous and prayerful about landing the internship, only to be told I was capable of being more. Mr. Wise saw an attorney inside of me. I almost felt like I was sitting in Ms. Gideon's office all over again. Mr. Wise was now the third person who saw more in me than I initially saw in myself.

I sat there and thought for a moment. I had previously contemplated law school on several occasions, but I had always quickly dismissed the idea for several reasons. For starters, I wasn't certain I could make the commitment to three years of law school, while juggling my parental responsibilities. I also had financial concerns: I thought it would be too expensive. So, once again, I quickly dismissed the thought.

Finally, I asked, "Am I still being considered for the paralegal intern position that I came to interview for?" He replied, "This will be the easiest interview you ever have, you have the internship position without question, no need for an interview. What you really need to do is seriously consider going to law school." I ended up interning for Mr. Wise for several months while completing my paralegal program.

Upon graduating from the program, I accepted a paralegal position with a foreclosure law firm. While working there, I continued to periodically entertain the thought of attending law school. As a paralegal, I did most of the legal work for the attorneys. I drafted legal documents and assisted the attorneys by preparing the foreclosure file from beginning to end. The attorney would take the completed legal file and make the necessary motions and court appearances. My job was routine and mundane. I was not being mentally challenged or fulfilled. I prepared the same paperwork for a different client day after day.

That particular firm also didn't offer much growth opportunity for a paralegal. The most I could do there was to become a paralegal supervisor. As a paralegal, I could never appear in court or actually represent a client. I was limited to assisting the attorneys in preparing the cases.

Having ignited my drive trait, my future as a paralegal became less and less appealing, and law school was becoming more and more appealing. I was still hesitant about the commitment, though. However, when I started discussing my interest in "someday" attending law school with the attorneys I worked for, surprisingly, they encouraged me to apply. They even agreed to write my letters of recommendation.

I ended up becoming so consumed with the idea of attending law school that it began to affect my paralegal work. I started to lose interest in my job. I was constantly researching law schools and discussing my law school interest and concerns with my co-workers.

One day, one of the supervising attorneys called me into his office. He said, "You don't seem happy here."

Well I wasn't completely happy there, so I sarcastically replied, "Happiness is not a job requirement." I sincerely felt like I was just there to perform a job and collect a pay check. I knew intuitively that I was playing it small there as a paralegal, but the chatter in my head kept saying, "Law school is too long, too expensive, too hard for a parent with a young child." That, and so many more pessimistic thoughts, kept repeating in my head, causing me to keep dismissing law school as an option.

My supervising attorney suggested I pursue law school. This was a nice way of saying, "You are fired."

I had mixed emotions. I was concerned because I had a son to provide for, so I needed a job. But on the other hand, I wasn't really happy being a paralegal. I was beginning to realize I had settled on that career. I let the negative chatter in my head prevent me from seriously considering law school.

I began to contemplate my next move. I could have let that termination distress me, but I began to look at it as an opportunity. I realized that I could do anything I wanted now. I was jobless, but I still had a college degree, skills, and options. This termination was my opportunity to do something greater.

<u>One Door Closes but a Better Door Opens</u>

I had come to a crossroad in my life and didn't know which direction to go. Should I get another paralegal job—maybe a more fulfilling one? Should I get a job in business or accounting? Should I pursue law school? Those were the questions I kept asking myself.

I began to examine my life and the life coaches I had encountered along the way. I thought about my physical therapist encouraging me to face my situation. No matter how bleak and painful moving forward seemed, she always encouraged me to push through the discomfort. I then recalled Ms. Gideon, my guidance counselor, forcing me to reflect on my life and my future goals. She encouraged me to strive for better. Then I remembered Mr. Wise, the bankruptcy attorney I interned for, telling me the first time he met me that I should be in law school and that the law profession needs more lawyers like me. I then reflected upon that business law class that I took my last year in college. That was where I first developed an interest in the law. I had enjoyed that class tremendously. I also reflected on my brother's federal trial that I watched so intensely, all the while thinking I would be a much better lawyer than the one I observed representing him.

I identified and ignited my optimism character trait. I decided I was not "fired" but "released" to go on to a better opportunity. I saw the glass half full, not half empty. One door closed, so a better one could open. What looked like a setback was the set up to my new destined future. I was ready to exit the old mundane life as a paralegal—where my opportunities were limited—and enter my new exciting life, ultimately as an attorney with limitless opportunities.

Once I ignited my optimism character trait, I began to view my life differently. I turned off that negative chatter in my head, became optimistic, and started analyzing things from a positive perspective. For example, I used to say to myself, "It would take three years to finish law school, and that is a long time." But after igniting my optimism trait, I began to say, "The time is going to pass by anyway, so I may as well spend the next three years making something productive out of my life." I also used to think that "law school will be too hard." Instead, I began to think, "Anything worth having is worth working for, and nothing is too hard." I used to think that "law school will be too expensive." Instead, I began to think that "failure, regret, and unhappiness are more expensive."

After changing my perspective and thought process, I decided to apply to law school and pursue a career as an attorney.

Ignite Your Power

When you receive bad news, such as a termination notice, identify and ignite your optimism character trait. Evaluate the situation and ask yourself, "Was I truly happy in that situation or in that place? Am I destined to do something greater than I was doing? Was I playing it too small?" Reassess your goals, and take the next step toward those goals. Be optimistic about what your future holds. Eliminate the negative self-chatter in your head, and start thinking positively and optimistically. Your setback could be your set up.

Being released from my paralegal position turned out to be a blessing. When I worked there, I was playing it small. I was destined for so much more. My release forced me to find and ignite my optimism trait and to ultimately step into better opportunities. If you are laid off or fired, consider yourself released from that position for a very good reason. Perhaps you were in a stagnant place, maybe you were settling or playing your career small, or maybe you were contemplating opening a business or making a career change, but the negative chatter was holding you back. If you are presented with a release situation, learn to ignite your optimism character trait. Welcome the closing of that door so you can embrace the opportunities awaiting you behind a better door. Be optimistic, and soar!

Chapter 4: Open-Mindedness

> *Have you ever had an opportunity to do something but were too limited in your mindset to consider the opportunity? Thought, "I would have to travel too far?" "I would have to relocate?" "I would have to be too far away from my family and friends?" "I would have to start over?"*
>
> *If you answered "yes" to any of these questions, you need to identify and ignite your **"open-mindedness**" character trait!*

Application Denied

"Your LSAT score is too low"

I felt so optimistic. After being released from my paralegal job, I thought that I could now pursue my dream of becoming a lawyer. I still lived in New Jersey and had a son to support. All my family ties were in New Jersey, so clearly, I wanted to attend either Rutgers Law School (preferably the Newark location, but Camden was also an option) or Seton Hall Law School.

I took a Law School Admission Test (LSAT) prep course but still scored low on my LSATs. I took the actual LSAT a few times but still couldn't score higher. I applied to nearly 20 law schools, and even with my 3.0 GPA, the rejection letters kept rolling in because of my low LSAT scores. Rutgers Newark and many of the other schools I applied to had not accepted me. I hadn't received a response yet from Seton Hall Law.

One day in the midst of receiving several law school rejection letters, I received a letter from a law school I never heard of—Thomas M. Cooley Law School in Lansing, Michigan. The letter invited me to apply for admission. It also included an admission index formula so I could do a simple calculation based on my GPA and my LSAT score to determine if I would be accepted. If my number ranked above a certain given number, I would be guaranteed admission. So I did the calculation and appeared certain to be accepted at this school, with the potential of receiving a scholarship!

So, after being rejected by most of the law schools I had applied to, I thought that this unknown school was my only viable option. But it was in Michigan. I had never been to Michigan. I also had no friends or family in Michigan to act as a support system for me and Lamar, so I decided to discuss this opportunity with a few relatives. I remember that most of the lackadaisical ones said, "Michigan is too cold, it's too far, it's too this, it's too that..." Blah, blah blah. Not an encourager in sight.

Then, I spoke to my Uncle B. (O'Neil McPherson, Jr.), God bless his soul. I didn't grow up near my Uncle B. nor did I have a relationship with him when I was younger, but he became an integral part of my life when I was in college. He was the most open-minded person I knew.

He said, "Michigan is just a plane ride away." He believed in pursing dreams and thinking outside the box. He would always tell me that the world is huge and doesn't begin and end with New Jersey. Uncle B. was a traveler. He loved exploring the world and was the only person in my family who was living life on his own terms. When he became a part of my life, he truly inspired me. He is the person who encouraged me to get my real estate license and tax training when I was in college. He was a licensed realtor, too, and he believed in creating opportunities for wealth, even though some of those opportunities lie outside of your comfort zone. He wanted me to finish college, but he also encouraged me to acquire as many skills as possible along the way. He excelled at giving sound advice and was always supportive.

Uncle B. suggested that I visit Michigan and the law school, and if, after the visit, I liked the school and the environment for myself and Lamar, I should go for it. I took his advice. I ignited my open-mindedness character trait! I mailed my application. I then planned and prepared for a trip to Michigan, booking a three-day stay near the law school, and headed to the Midwest with Lamar.

From Thinking Small to Dreaming Big

Lamar and I arrived for our visit to Michigan with my open-mindedness trait blazing. I was prepared to explore as much as possible. We visited the law school, an apartment community, a local church, the movies, and some recreational facilities. I researched the various schools that Lamar could attend and different neighborhoods that we could live in. We made the most out of this three-day period and enjoyed the visit. I was certain that I would get the legal education I desired in an environment that appeared family-oriented and had an excellent school system for Lamar. A few weeks after returning from my visit, I received an acceptance letter. After contemplating my recent visit, I decided to relocate to Michigan with Lamar and attend Thomas M. Cooley Law School.

I was ready to pursue my dream of becoming a lawyer. I realized that I would continue to play it small if I disregarded Michigan as an option just because of the location and factors unrelated to my ultimate goal, so when the time came, I packed our entire life up in a U-Haul truck and headed to the Midwest to begin law school.

I recall finally receiving a letter from Seton Hall Law School in Newark when I was packing to move. It was a contingent acceptance, containing an offer for me to attend a pre-law school admission program. Basically, I could take legal classes over the summer at Seton Hall Law School, and if I did well, I would be offered admission for the fall. However, if I did not do well, I would be denied admission. I remembered hearing a horror story from a classmate in my undergraduate program at Rutgers. She had attended one of those programs at a different law school and complained that she had a difficult professor for one class and ultimately failed out of the program. As a result, she couldn't get into any other law school afterward because the schools considered her failure of the summer program as an indication of her inability to succeed in a full program.

I did not want that to happen, so I decided to accept a guaranteed law school admission over a contingent one. I knew I would work hard once at Thomas M. Cooley Law School ("Cooley"), so if I ever needed or wanted to transfer, my law school grades would be the new measuring point for my law school success at another school, not my LSAT score or a contingent summer program results.

We left New Jersey and settled in at our new place in Michigan. Lamar transitioned well, and so did I. We both made new friends, and we both did well in school.

During my first semester of law school, I made the dean's list and received several other honors, including an academic scholarship and an invitation to become a member of the Law Review. I didn't regret my decision to relocate. In fact, I thought it was one of the best decisions of my life. Igniting my open-mindedness character trait had truly paid off.

Ignite Your Power

If you are blessed with an opportunity to achieve a goal but that opportunity requires you to relocate or do something outside of your initial expectations or plans, ignite your open-mindedness character trait. Your opportunity to achieve your dream or goals may not be behind the door you expect it to be. It might be in another state or another country, for that matter. You have to be willing to explore opportunities outside of the box.

Remember: nothing grows in a comfort zone. If you want to grow, you may have to uproot yourself and replant yourself where the ground is more fertile (more opportunities). Therefore, be open-minded about all existing possibilities, and sincerely evaluate them. You are only restricted by limitations you place on yourself, so remove those limiting thoughts, be open-minded, and achieve all that you set out to achieve. Be open-minded, and soar!

Chapter 5: Persistence

> *Have you ever really needed or wanted something and were told "no"? Been told that no more applications are being considered? Been told no more grants or scholarships are available? Been told no more funds are available? No more slots available? No more vacancies?*
>
> *If you answered "yes" to any of these questions, or similar ones, and you accepted "no" as the final answer, you may need to identify and ignite your **"persistence"** character trait.*

Not Accepted

"Sorry, We are not Accepting Walk-in Applications"

I had completed my first semester at Cooley Law School, was on the dean's list, and had received an academic scholarship. Lamar had transitioned well, was making lots of new friends, and had joined his school basketball team. He was thriving in his new environment. But, things soon changed.

During my second semester, I became ill. I was hospitalized and needed emergency surgery, so my family was called to Michigan. While I waited on my family to arrive, my law school friends stepped in to help care for Lamar, who was now in the 7th grade. After my family came, I had my surgery and was later released from the hospital to recuperate at home. After this ordeal, my family and I thought it would be better if I moved closer to home.

Prior to my illness, I had contemplated transferring to a higher ranking law school at the end of my first year. My initial goal was to get into an American Bar Association–approved law school, do well, and then possibly transfer to a higher ranking law school because my admission on my transfer application would be based solely upon my grades, not my LSAT scores.

My illness caused me to reconsider the idea a little sooner, especially if I could move back to New Jersey. Cooley Law School operated on a trimester system—unlike other law schools, which operate with two semesters per school year—so students attend class all year round with a two-week break in between each semester. At the end of my second semester, I planned to return to New Jersey to visit my family during my two-week break.

While in New Jersey, I started talking with Mr. Dynasty (A.J. Nolton) about my desire to transfer law schools. Mr. Dynasty was my confidant and true sounding board. He is the ultimate visionary. He doesn't just think outside the box; he lives outside the box. He suggested that I visit Rutgers Law School and Seton Hall Law School and seek admission.

I thought he was insane. I explained to him that you don't just walk into a school and ask to be admitted—it wasn't an emergency room. He said, "You can ask for whatever you want. The worst that can happen is you get a 'no.'"

I thought about it and decided to be bold. I planned to visit Rutgers Law School and Seton Hall Law School in Newark, in person, and seek admission as a transfer applicant. Heck, I had nothing to lose. I had contemplated transferring, but I didn't want to be rash and withdraw from my current law school with no definitive answer that I would be accepted as a transfer student somewhere else. So why not explore my admission options while in New Jersey?

I stopped by Rutgers Law School

first. I marched directly to the admissions office and sought admission. If I couldn't get a definitive answer, I was hoping for an indication of whether my transfer application would be approved. Rutgers refused to entertain my bold "verbal request" and advised me to submit a formal written application and wait for a decision in the mail. I explained that I only had a two-week break and really needed an indication that my application would be accepted. They reiterated the application process. I wasn't surprised, but I was still disappointed after getting my hopes up that I might actually be considered. With that denial, I left.

I then marched over to Seton Hall Law School to try my luck there. I was told the same thing. I was advised to submit a formal application and wait for a response in the mail. I once again explained my circumstances, but the secretary at the admission desk continued to deny my request. However, her desk was right outside the dean of admissions' office, and he happened to be in his office at the time. He apparently heard me pleading my case to his secretary.

I was igniting my "persistence" trait! Things began to change.

No to Yes

After overhearing me persistently plead my case, the dean of admissions came out of his office—most likely to see who the crazy person was who wasn't taking "no" for an answer. He then invited me into his office.

Perhaps the dean was planning to let me down graciously in private. He began to explain the application process, advising me that my application must be in writing and that the decision would arrive in writing through the mail. He further explained that several weeks might pass before I would receive a response.

Then, I explained my situation directly to him. I told him that I needed to be closer to home and that I had excelled during my first year of law school. I informed him that I was on the dean's list both my first and second semester, was the recipient of several awards, and had been invited to be a member of Law Review (membership is limited to those who achieved high academic excellence). I tried everything to convince him to at least give me an informal acceptance so I could make arrangements to transfer within the next two weeks.

Again, he tried to gently turn me down, saying that he couldn't make such a decision on the spot. He went on to explain all the factors involved in the decision-making process. One would be a review of my transcripts to see how well I was performing at my current law school.

I interrupted him. "Good thing I came prepared!" I whipped out my transcripts and handed them to him. He seemed shocked that I had them with me.

After seeing my grades, the dean took me more seriously. My grades were stellar. They were a clear indication that I was performing exceptionally. He was familiar with Cooley Law School and knew that it was pretty easy to get into but extremely difficult to graduate from. The attrition rate at Cooley Law was around 20% at that time. Therefore, he was impressed that I was doing so well. He seemed equally impressed with my relentless pitch for an "on the spot" admission decision despite the fact that I was told "no" multiple times.

After listening to my persistent request, witnessing how prepared I was, and perhaps thinking I would, in fact, make a great lawyer as I was already pleading—and seemed to be winning—my first case, the dean said "You can advise your school that you are transferring."

Yes! I was ecstatic. Then he added, "I need you to submit a formal application; this is an informal acceptance. I don't usually do this, but I can tell you I'm pretty certain you will be accepted."

I was extremely grateful that my persistence had paid off, but I had one additional problem: I had no money, so I couldn't afford Seton Hall Law School. Seton Hall was more expensive than Cooley, and I had a scholarship at Cooley. I was prepared to plead my second case—I needed some financial assistance.

I had to convince the dean that I was not only deserving of admission, but admission with a scholarship. I began to plead my second case. I explained that I was receiving an academic scholarship from Cooley Law School and that I had a son to provide for. I told him that it would be practically impossible to transfer to Seton Hall Law School without being granted a scholarship, but the dean firmly stated that transfer students do not qualify for scholarships.

I had already ignited my persistence trait, so I wasn't giving up now. I pleaded my case some more and was ultimately able to convince the dean that I deserved a scholarship. He told me to write an essay explaining my situation and give it to him ASAP. Again, he indicated that he couldn't promise anything, but he was pretty certain that scholarship money would be made available to me. Mission accomplished.

I was able to turn that "no" to admission and "no" to a scholarship into a "yes" because I was persistent. My persistence resulted in acceptance and scholarship money.

<u>Ignite Your Power</u>

The key to getting what you need and want in life is persistence. You cannot just accept "no" for an answer. The old adage, "Ask and you shall receive," is true. If you truly want something, you have to go after it relentlessly with unwavering persistence. Ignite your persistence trait whenever you hear "no" but you know that you truly deserve and/or desperately need whatever you are pursuing. Be persistent, and soar!

Chapter 6: Motivation

*Have you ever applied for your dream job and been told, "Sorry the position has been filled"? Applied for a loan and been told your bank application was denied? If you answered "yes" to any of these questions and as a result, were left feeling disappointed and disenchanted, you need to identify and ignite your **"motivation"** character trait!*

The Position Has Been Filled

"We Regret to Inform You that We Cannot Offer You a Position"

I was accepted to Seton Hall Law School as a transfer student and received a scholarship and some financial aid. During my senior year, I signed up for Career Day to secure a job upon graduating. I also signed up for a mock interview program where I was assigned an attorney from a law firm to interview and critique me. The mock interview program allowed graduating seniors an opportunity to practice interviewing with real attorneys at real law firms before actually interviewing for an attorney position. Students would set up an interview appointment with the mentor attorney at his or her law firm and then, at the respective time, appear dressed and prepared as if the student were actually interviewing for a real position.

An attorney at a midsized New Jersey law firm mentored me for my mock interview. It was beneficial, and I received excellent feedback. I was ready for Career Day. When the signup sheet was posted for the participating law firms and government agencies, I was excited to see the firm that I participated in the mock interview with on the list, so I eagerly signed up to interview with that firm. I also signed up for an interview with the Drug Enforcement Agency (DEA), another small law firm, and the District Attorney's (DA's) Office from Philadelphia.

When Career Day came, I proceeded through all the interviews I had lined up. I was particularly interested in the midsize New Jersey law firm, and I believed I had nailed the interview. Besides, I felt like I had an advantage, having previously mock interviewed with an attorney from the same firm who coached me on how to successfully interview. Although I interviewed with the other three entities, I had no interest in working for them. I wanted to work at that midsized firm.

After my interviews, I assessed my thoughts more intensely. I determined that the DEA was completely out of consideration. I had no desire to participate in undercover drug sting operations and dangerous assignments. The small law firm was out because it seemed too boutique. I didn't give much consideration to the DA's Office from Philadelphia because up until my interview, I didn't realize that a "district attorney" was the same thing as a "prosecutor." In New Jersey we do not use the term "district attorney."

Prior to my interview with the Philadelphia DA's Office, I never contemplated becoming a part of law enforcement because I came from an inner city neighborhood where a huge divide lay between the citizens and law enforcement due to disparities in the treatment of minorities and non-minorities in the criminal justice system. In fact, my interview with the DA's Office occurred during a peak in tensions in America between minorities and law enforcement.

A concealed racial profiling policy enacted by the New Jersey State Police had just come to public attention and was making headlines across the nation. In April 1998, a van traveling on the New Jersey Turnpike with four young men inside—one Hispanic and the other three black—was stopped by two state troopers who alleged that the van was speeding. That traffic stop resulted in those two state troopers firing 11 shots into the van, injuring three of the occupants, two severely. None of the men inside were armed. This case became New Jersey's most explosive racial profiling case, and it brought national attention to the racial profiling policy enacted by the New Jersey State Troopers, specifically targeted at stopping minority motorists. "D.W.B." (driving while black) became common household terminology in minority communities. Racial tensions were at an all-time high.

During my interview with the Philadelphia DA's Office, I recall being asked how I felt about that seminal racial profiling case. I knew that this case had been highly publicized across the nation, but similar incidents were so commonplace in my community that I hadn't given this particular incident any greater thought.

Because I hadn't prepared for this interview or this line of questioning, I simply responded truthfully and from the heart. In sum, I responded that every profession has good and bad people, and that includes police departments. Although we cannot hold an entire profession accountable for those few "bad apples," measures have to be taken and polices implemented to expose and get rid of those "bad apples." Simultaneous measures have to be implemented to increase the presence of the "good apples." In addition, policies have to be fair across the board and uniformly enforced and applied. The interview went well, and it proceeded with similar types of questions.

I recall developing a good rapport with my interviewer, M.K. Feeney. I enjoyed interviewing with her, and I left feeling really good about the interview. But again, I hadn't given much thought at that time to becoming a prosecutor. I also recall that at the end of the interview, M.K. Feeney gave me a pamphlet describing the District Attorney's Office and the duties of an assistant district attorney (ADA). I slipped the pamphlet into my bag as I left the interview.

When I got home, I was so excited about my interview at the midsize firm because I just knew I nailed it. I couldn't wait to get my "You are Hired" letter. When I began to clean out my bag before retiring for the evening, I came across the brochure M.K. Feeney gave me about the Philadelphia DA's Office. Without reading it, I flicked the pamphlet into my waste basket.

A few days later, I received a letter in the mail from the midsize law firm. I couldn't wait to tear open the envelope. The letter read:

"Sorry, after careful consideration we regret to inform you that we cannot offer you a position with our firm at this time."

I was devastated. That was the job I wanted. I sat for a moment, thinking about what I should do next. I wanted "that" job but I needed "a" job upon graduating. I had a son to feed. After moping around feeling discouraged, I thought about how far I had come. I had to ignite my motivation character trait!

The pity party was soon over. I started reconsidering my other options. I was adamant about not becoming a DEA, and I really didn't want to work at that boutique law firm. What about the DA's Office in Philadelphia? Although I never considered becoming an ADA, I did enjoy my interview with M.K. Feeney. I thought that if that office was as pleasant as she was, it would actually be a great place to work. I began to consider the ADA position as a possible career option.

I rummaged through my wastebasket and pulled out the brochure that I had quickly discarded a few days earlier. For the first time, I read the job description for an ADA: I would be in court every day advocating on behalf of victims of crime in the City of Philadelphia. I would conduct preliminary hearings, motions, and trials. I would develop trial skills. So far, the position seemed appealing. I continued to read the pamphlet. The more I read, the more intrigued I became.

Then I thought about that disconnect between minorities and law enforcement. If I served as an ADA, I could give the citizens of Philadelphia a voice they could trust inside law enforcement. As a product of the inner city, I could relate to their circumstances and their interactions with police. I would be that "good apple," I would conduct my duties with honesty and integrity, and I would hold anyone that I came into contact with, including the police, accountable for operating under the same standards. Serving as an ADA could help me bridge that disconnect. I could address the disparities in the cases I was responsible for, and I would hold myself accountable to the community for exercising fair and uniform treatment for all offenders. I realized this may in fact be a great opportunity for both me and the community I would be serving.

The next day I received a letter in

the mail inviting me to Philadelphia for a second interview with a panel of district attorneys. I had never been to Philadelphia, but I remembered my experience when I contemplated moving to Michigan. I recalled how wonderful that relocation was and how that experience turned out to be a great opportunity. I decided to travel to Philadelphia for the second panel interview.

I contacted my free chauffer, Poppadoppalis. He was familiar with Philadelphia and agreed to drive me. The panel interview went well—I later learned that I nailed it. I answered the questions honestly and from the heart, just as I did in my first interview with M.K. Feeney. A week or so later, I received a job offer in the mail. After careful consideration, I eagerly accepted the position of Assistant District Attorney for the City of Philadelphia and looked forward to working there upon graduating law school.

Disappointment to Destiny

I recall how disappointed I was when I wasn't hired for the attorney position with that midsize New Jersey law firm—the position that I initially thought was my dream job. But that disappointment is what motivated me to explore other career options. Had I been offered that job, I may have deferred my destiny. Working at that midsized law firm would have been similar to working at the foreclosure law firm, except I would have been the lawyer preparing the file, not the paralegal. Most first and second year attorneys in firms never see a courtroom. I would have been consumed preparing files and billing hours.

Being an ADA was an opportunity to become a change agent: work with victims of crime, bridge the gap between law enforcement and the community, prosecute offenders, ensure cases were prosecuted fairly with honesty and integrity, and most importantly, positively impact the lives of others in the community. At the same time, I would be developing valuable skills. I would learn to think on my feet, advocate effectively, and hone my trial skills, all while serving as the much needed voice for the citizens of Philadelphia. Little did I know then that this position would align me with my destiny. I was about to become a servant leader, while discovering my true gifts and talents. It was that disappointing letter from the midsize New Jersey law firm that led me to explore alternatives. Exploring those alternatives led me down the path to my destiny.

Ignite Your Power

If you ever feel disappointed because you didn't get the job or the promotion you wanted, don't get discouraged. Ignite your motivation character trait, and find your next opportunity. Life doesn't have accidents or coincidences. Everything happens for a reason. The job or promotion you want so badly may not be best for you. It may not be aligned with your destiny. Our heavenly father works everything out for our good. He doesn't always give us what we want, but he always gives us what we need.

Your destiny may be tied to a disappointment. That's why you have to stay motivated and move forward. So, if receiving disappointing news leads you to wallow in self-pity instead of motivating you to move forward, you may miss out on the blessing that's waiting for you. Whenever life throws you a curve ball, adapt, stay motivated, and move forward. Motivation will propel you to where your destiny lies. Get motivated, and soar!

Chapter 7: Self-Worth & Self-Esteem

> *Have you ever had a negative experience that caused you to doubt yourself? Doubt your skill and talents? Caused you to remain stagnant?*
>
> *If you answered "yes" to any of these questions, you need to identify and ignite your **"self-worth/self-esteem"** character trait.*

No Promotion

"A Budget Freeze has Resulted in no Hiring and, Thus, no Promotions"

Upon graduating from Seton Hall Law School, I relocated to Philadelphia to begin my career as an ADA. I started in the Municipal Court Unit.

I loved my job and learned a lot as a trial attorney, all while serving the citizens of Philadelphia. I was in court every day conducting preliminary hearings, motions, and trials. I discharged my duties with honesty and integrity.

A typical day involved prosecuting about 30 cases that were usually split between me and my trial partner. It was a lot of work, but it was very rewarding. I interacted and formed relationships with victims, police officers, detectives, witnesses, defense attorneys, law clerks, and judges, and I gained respect from all of those individuals.

Typically, an ADA is initially assigned to the Municipal Court Unit. Afterward, you progress to the Juvenile Unit, then to the Felony Waiver Unit. After that, an ADA is likely to progress on to either the Major Trial Unit or a specialized unit such as the Family Violence/Sexual Assault Unit, the Repeat Offender Unit, and then, ultimately, the Homicide Unit. When an ADA initially accepts the position, it is usually with the expectation of rotating through the Municipal Court Unit, followed by Felony Waiver and Juvenile Units, respectively, each in about 6 to 12 months. The goal is to get through those three units so you can serve in either the Major Trial Unit or a specialized unit like the Family Violence or Homicide Unit for the remainder of your career at the office.

During the time spent in the Municipal Court, Felony Waiver, and Juvenile Units, an ADA hones their trial skills. However, being assigned to any of those units for more than a year can become frustrating because an ADA generally masters all there is to master in a particular unit within that time frame. This can cause the ADA to feel dissatisfied.

At one point while I was assigned to the Municipal Court Unit, the office had a hiring freeze, and it didn't help that my incoming ADA class was large. Those factors, coupled with office politics, meant extremely slow promotions for many of us.

I remained in the Municipal Court Unit for nearly two years. Although I enjoyed my job, I eventually started to question my skill, talent, and self-worth because I had learned all I could in the Municipal Court Unit and was no longer being challenged. I thought that my promotion wasn't coming soon enough, but rather than allow my self–esteem to take a dive, I identified and ignited my self-worth/self-esteem character trait.

I decided that I was in a "delayed" stage of my career. I was being delayed—not denied—a promotion. I wanted to remain with the DA's Office and gain all the trial experience I possibly could. And I knew a promotion was ultimately coming, so resigning would have been premature and impulsive. It wasn't a sensible option at that time. However, I also realized that I needed to do something while in this delayed stage to address the lack of self-worth that was starting to set in. I decided that I wouldn't sit back and wait on a promotion to enhance my trial skills and validate my self-worth. It was time that I took responsibility and action for my own self-development.

Stagnant to Self-Development

While appearing to be stuck in the Municipal Court Unit, I learned about a program offered at Temple Law School that some of the seasoned trial attorneys at the DA's Office had attended. It was a trial advocacy program that allowed lawyers to earn a master's degree in trial advocacy (an LL.M). I researched the program and spoke to several of the trial attorneys in the DA's Office's Homicide Unit who had successfully completed the program. Every trial attorney I spoke to raved about the benefits of the program, including how it helped them vastly improve their trial skills. I decided to apply to the program. I submitted my application, in addition to the gleaming recommendations that many of the seasoned trial attorneys wrote on my behalf.

I was accepted into the program and excitedly began my new pursuit. Enrolling in the LL.M Trial Advocacy Program was the perfect solution to addressing my outlook. I had felt like my career was stagnant, despite knowing that I had skills and talents. I was confident the LL.M Program would relieve the feeling of complacency that was beginning to set in while allowing me to enhance both my education and trial skills. At the end of the program, I would have additional trial experience and a master's degree: a win–win situation. Moreover, I wouldn't have to rely on the DA's Office and/or a promotion to enhance my personal career development. I had taken matters into my own hands.

You may not be able to control how other people value you, but you can control how you value yourself and how you deal with complacency in your life. I discovered and ignited my self-worth/self-esteem character trait and attended the LL.M Program, graduating from Temple

Law School with an LL.M in Trial Advocacy, with honors. After I was finally promoted at the DA's Office, I applied what I learned in the LL.M Program to my first jury trial, which I won with a favorable verdict in less than 30 minutes. My self-worth/self-esteem was at an all-time high because of the action I took, not something or someone else.

Ignite Your Power

You can't let a job, other people, or a promotion define your self-worth, your level of self-esteem, or your validation. If your career has become stagnate or you feel complacent, you have to find a way to become fulfilled. You also cannot let someone or something else be responsible for your self-development and your self-growth.

If you ever find yourself in a similar situation, explore your options for personal development. Don't be afraid to explore opportunities outside of your place of employment. Resigning is not always the best solution. There is a time and place for everything.

Maybe, like in my situation, you are in a "delay" stage in your career or at your job: promotion is expected to come, but it just isn't coming fast enough. Or perhaps, another position is about to open up soon, and you are trying to hold out for it. Whatever the reason, if you are in a "delay" season, resigning may not be practical; however, it is always the perfect time to enhance your training and skill set so when it is time to move on, you will have the requisite skill, experience, and education necessary for success in your next venture. Obtain all the training and experience your current job has to offer before moving on.

You may be confident that that promotion, new position, or new business venture will eventually come, but that doesn't mean you have to sit by idly waiting for that change while your self-esteem is being compromised. In your delayed season, be proactive, and find ways outside of your job to satisfy that desire to be completely self-fulfilled, while maintaining your employment. Don't let that delay validate you. Ignite your own self-worth/self–esteem trait, and soar!

Chapter 8: Faith

Have you ever been in a situation where you felt it was time to take your business or an opportunity to the next level, but you were not certain if you would succeed despite the fact that you were qualified? Ever been afraid to walk away from job security even though you were not happy with the job? Afraid to let go of a steady paycheck, even though your paycheck is not enough?

*If you answered "yes" to any of these questions, you need to identify and ignite your **"faith"** character trait!*

What's Next?

"It's Time to Move On"

Soon after enrolling in the LL.M program, my delay season ended. I was promoted to the Juvenile Unit and remained there for about a year. I was then promoted to the Felony Waiver Unit, followed by the Major Trial Unit. After working in the Major Trial Unit for about a year—having conducted numerous jury trials and earning my LL.M in trial advocacy—I knew it was time to move on.

I was confident that I had gained the requisite education, skill, knowledge, and experience necessary to open my own law firm. I began to reflect on all my legal experience, including my experience as a paralegal. I began to assess my skill set.

I had participated in the Family Law Clinic during my first semester of my last year of law school. There, I represented clients with family law matters as a student attorney. I drafted various legal documents and litigated matters in court on their behalf, under the guidance and supervision of an attorney. I participated in the Criminal Law Clinic my second semester of my last year of law school. In that position, I interviewed persons who had recently been accused of crimes and arrested and were awaiting bail hearings. I advocated on behalf of those defendants in court to get them either released on their own recognizance or nominal bail. I was a paralegal before law school and had attained both bankruptcy and real estate legal experience. As a licensed attorney, I had been an ADA for nearly four years and had prosecuted thousands of criminal matters and conducted numerous jury trials.

I surmised that I had experience in family law, bankruptcy law, real estate law, and criminal law. I was satisfied that I had attained the proper foundation necessary to establish a successful private law practice.

However, like most people, I was pretty comfortable receiving my small stipend of a paycheck every two weeks. It didn't seem to be much, but at least it was consistent. Like most people, I appreciated the stability of my job. I continued to contemplate opening my own law practice, but my biggest concern was the uncertainty of success and the financial risk involved, especially considering I had parental responsibilities.

Then one morning while driving to court, I received a call on my cell phone from one of the football coaches from Syracuse University, Coach White. He said, "Hello, Ms. McPherson, How would you like to receive $27,000 a year?" I replied, "What? Let me pull over." After I pulled my car to the side of the road, I continued my conversation with Coach White. He continued, "We would like to offer your son a full scholarship to Syracuse University valued at approximately $27,000 a year."

Lamar was a senior in high school and a football star. Many colleges were seeking to recruit him. Needless to say, Syracuse was the first to make an official offer. This was great news, and it could not have come at a more perfect time. I was concerned about walking away from job security, knowing that I had a mouth at home to feed, but knowing that Lamar's education, housing, and meals would be taken care of for the next four years allowed me to seriously consider taking a leap of faith into private practice. I figured if private practice didn't work out, it would just be me sleeping on the park bench, not me and my son. After carefully considering the risks and benefits, I decided to step out on faith. I resigned from the DA's Office.

Employed to Self-Employed

On June 11, 2005, I started my own firm and went into private law practice. My primary practice area was criminal defense, but I practiced in several other areas as well. I found my practice rewarding.

I will never forget my first trial in private practice: it was a murder trial. After starting my private practice career with that trial, I thought that every other case to follow would be easy. Nothing could be more serious than a murder case with a client facing life in prison. Every case after that was accepted with ease. For the first ten years in private practice, I was fulfilled. I enjoyed advocating for my clients. I particularly enjoyed defending the wrongfully accused and fighting for those deserving compensation for injuries resulting from negligent conduct.

Serving as the voice of those whose voices are often unheard and whose faith in the system has been shattered is rewarding. I recall representing an individual wrongfully accused of kidnapping, robbery, and assault. He faced a minimum of 30 years in prison. He sat in jail, unable to afford his exorbitant bail. And although he had a rock solid alibi, he had very little faith in the integrity of the criminal justice system because he knew of similar cases where injustice and disparity resulted. He had also been consulting with the attorneys in the orange jumpsuits—his fellow inmates—and getting their "expert" opinions. As a result, he wanted to plead guilty just to get out of jail. Unfortunately, this isn't uncommon in the criminal justice system.

I had to convince him to reject all plea offers and trust me to get him vindicated. I reminded my client that I actually had a law degree, unlike his so-called "expert" fellow inmates, and I was confident—based on the facts of his case and the law—that I would prevail. He was reluctant to challenge the criminal justice system, but he finally trusted me to deliver justice. As he sat in jail, I fought vigorously on his behalf. Through thorough investigation and perseverance, I was able to get him vindicated, without the necessity of a trial. His case was ultimately dismissed, and he walked out of jail a free man.

I recall another matter where my working-class clients were being cheated out of overtime pay. I represented them in a class action lawsuit and was victorious in getting them all of the compensation that they were cheated out of and so desperately needed and deserved. These types of cases bring me the most satisfaction. In these cases, justice was served, and I knew I had positively impacted the lives of others.

However some cases don't bring the same type of satisfaction, despite the fact that they are pursued and/or defended with the same zeal and vigor. I have defended people charged with heinous crimes with insurmountable evidence such as DNA, video surveillance, or confessions describing gruesome details. Those cases can be challenging, but I enjoy challenges and have been successful in many of these types of cases, as well, so the challenge never bothers me. What bothers me most about many of these cases is the typical mindset of the offender. These offenders are usually under-privileged products of their environment. They often have limited resources and lack goals, education, self-respect, respect for others, and proper guidance. As a result, they often make poor decisions and bad choices that lead to criminal activity and, ultimately, jail. I am particularly bothered when the offender is young and could lose his freedom for the rest of his life because of a bad choice he made.

Whenever I have cases like this, I wonder if these offenders would have turned out differently if someone had prayed over their lives as hard as my grandmother prayed over mine. What if they had a life coach like my physical therapist who could have explained to them all the sacrifices others made for them so they could become great? Perhaps, they needed someone like Ms. Gideon in their lives, someone monitoring their decisions or their indecision; someone watching over them, ready to summon them in for a meeting to discuss the direction of their future based on their current actions or inaction; someone to engage them in a meaningful discussion about the importance of their choices and their future early in their lives. What if they had a John Wise in their lives—someone taking the initiative to examine their background and point out the potential they possess, especially when they don't recognize or appreciate that potential.

These burning questions brewed inside of me every time I represented such an offender. Practicing law is fulfilling, but private practice and my interactions with these types of young offenders began to awaken a deeper calling within me. Maybe I was being called to do more than just practice law. Perhaps I could use my voice to reach people who need guidance, either before they enter the criminal justice system or before they decide to give up along their journey in life. It turns out, my leap of faith from employed to self-employed led me on a journey to Purpose.

Ignite your Power

Faith is essential to life and Purpose. It is trusting and believing in a higher power and authority to bring forth unseen results. Those results are not guaranteed, but faith allows you to trust and believe that they will occur.

You must ignite your faith character trait whenever you face uncertainties in life. If you are seeking results that you have no proof will occur, because the results are outside of your power and control, you must ignite your faith trait.

When I decided to quit my job as an ADA to start my law practice, it was not guaranteed that my firm would be successful. I had to believe my firm would be successful by igniting my faith trait and trusting in the almighty God that I serve to bring forth that unpredictable result.

Remember, faith without work is dead. Therefore, you must lay a proper foundation so your faith can have a solid launching pad to ignite from.

Recall how I gained experience in law school clinics, as a paralegal, and as an ADA. I also obtained my LL.M to improve my education, training, and trial skills. Only after I put in the work and acquired the requisite skill set and proper education (a foundational launch pad for faith) did I ignite my faith trait.

Faith is not about neglecting your responsibilities or acting irresponsibly. Taking a leap of faith does not mean making sporadic decisions to chase your dreams or achieve your goals. It is about using your common sense and building a proper foundation for faith to attach to and ignite. Once you have laid that foundation by building your skill set and honing your gifts and talents, then you can ignite your faith by calling upon that higher power to bring forth the unforeseen fruits of your labor: *success*.

So, establish a foundational launch pad for your faith by putting in the necessary work. Then ignite your faith and soar!

Chapter 9: Purpose

Have you ever felt unfulfilled? Not completely satisfied with where you are in life? Felt like you should be getting more out of life? Felt like you aren't living up to your full potential? Felt like you should be doing more for others?

*If you answered "yes" to any of these questions, it's time to live in **Purpose!***

Not Completely Fulfilled

Those burning questions respecting those young offenders were still surfacing. I recall coming home from court one day and having a conversation with my cousin-grandmother, Mattie Brown about those lingering questions.

Mattie was my 85-year-old cousin and my grandmother's niece, God rest her soul. When my grandmother passed away, Mattie became a surrogate grandmother to both me and Lamar, so I began to refer to her as simply "my grandmother." During my last year of law school, Mattie became ill, and I became her caretaker. When I relocated to Philadelphia, I brought her with us. I remember that, when I first began caring for her, I thought it would be a lot of work. She was elderly and a disabled amputee, and I had so much on my plate. I refused to put her in a nursing home, though, so I accepted the responsibility.

While she stayed with us, I found so much comfort in my daily conversations with her. Through her words of encouragement and the uplifting stories she often shared, I felt like she was actually taking care of me. She once told me to live my life to the fullest, unapologetically. Mattie was a product of the Great Depression, so she worked hard her whole life and saved every penny, intending to travel the world after she retired. Before she retired, she never vacationed or got to do much of anything for herself. Unfortunately, she became ill soon after retiring and had to move in with me to be cared for, unable to travel or live any of the dreams she kept putting off. But despite her medical challenges and unfulfilled dreams, she was the happiest woman I knew. Her spirit was always positive and uplifting.

I enjoyed my conversations with Mattie; she inspired me with her life stories. I knew I wanted to be to others what Mattie was to me: an inspiration.

After talking to Mattie and carefully reflecting on some of those young offenders, I was convinced to take action and live my life to the fullest. I would not only practice law, but I would also speak to, mentor, and share my story with a broader segment of the community. I began to speak to youth groups, women's shelters, teenage mothers, and anyone whose lives I felt I could positively impact. My gift is that of a servant leader, charged with impacting the lives of as many people as I can reach.

The more I mentored, spoke, and encouraged people from all walks of life, the more I realized that for the past eleven years I was fulfilled, but I was not completely fulfilled. I truly enjoy practicing law, but I realized that people outside of the criminal justice system need to be poured into, too. People aren't just facing legal dilemmas; they are facing life dilemmas. I have had my share of life dilemmas, so I can relate. My Purpose is to use my education, training, and experience as an attorney to help those with legal issues, while also using my life experiences and my story to help empower those with life issues.

I have come to truly appreciate my journey. It has bought me to a place of complete fulfillment; it has brought me into my Purpose.

From Merely Existing to Living in Purpose

Often, we are consumed with living a mundane, routine life. We wake up, go to work, come home, engage in social media, have dinner with our family, maybe watch a little TV or read a book, and then retire for the night and repeat the same scenario day after day. It is time to stop merely existing and start living in your Purpose.

We all have a Purpose that has been pre-wired inside of us, and we each must discover our own. For the past eleven years, I thought I was living a pretty good life. I built a successful law practice and enjoyed being a trial attorney. I was content, but honestly, questions burned inside of me—like those about the young offenders—that made me realize I still wasn't living in my complete Purpose. I wasn't pouring into as many people as I could.

I learned through my life experiences that I have a much broader Purpose: to impact lives worldwide, not just in the legal sector. This realization resulted in the birth of this book so I could share my story. My Purpose stretches beyond the walls of the courthouse: my Purpose is to inspire and impact people across the globe. I am here to encourage everyone to soar beyond their adversities and to live a life of Purpose.

Start Walking in Your Purpose

Evaluate your journey, and begin to identify your Purpose. Your purpose is your calling—it's the gift you need to share with the world. It's that thing that is therapeutic to you, but inspiring to others. It brings you joy no matter what adversities it took to discover it. You must begin walking in purpose if you are to live a completely fulfilled life.

Chapter 10: S.O.A.R.

It's time to Soar!

S.O.A.R.—Soar Over Adversities Resiliently

Honing in on the 8 Character Traits that will Propel You to S.O.A.R.

The triumphs and adversities in your life strengthen your character. Though you will face various adversities throughout life, overcoming them depends on how you deal with those adversities when they show up. If you ignite the eight character traits that I had to ignite when faced with some of my personal adversities, you will soar over adversities resiliently! S.O.A.R.!

Recall how I ignited my eight character traits, and do the same: I ignited my **determination** trait to get me through a tragic accident and the physical challenge of learning to walk again. Ignite your determination trait whenever you are faced with a health condition, a medical diagnosis, a physical challenge, or any situation that requires you to decide that you will become determined and survive.

My **drive** trait was ignited when I needed to take action to pursue higher education and not settle for a mediocre life after learning I was a pregnant teenager. Ignite your drive trait when you feel unmotivated, you feel like settling, you feel lackadaisical, or you are faced with a draining situation. Put your drive into action, and press forward.

I ignited my **optimism** trait when I was terminated from my paralegal position. I saw that experience as me being "released" to pursue a greater calling: law school. Ignite your optimism trait whenever you get what seems to be bad news such as being fired, laid off, evicted, or even divorced. Use your optimism trait to help you see the glass as half full as opposed to half empty. Your optimism trait can change your mindset and help you see the positive lesson wrapped in a negative event.

I ignited my **open-mindedness** trait when my applications to local law schools were all denied. To pursue my dream, I had to consider moving to the Midwest. Use your open-mindedness trait to help you think outside the box and step outside your comfort zone. Remember, nothing grows inside a comfort zone, and your open-mindedness trait will help you see that. Use this trait when you are faced with a situation that requires you to stretch your viewpoint, such as when your job relocates, you get a business opportunity somewhere you didn't plan to live, you consider an unexpected temporary long-distance relationship, or any situation that causes you to consider factors you didn't initially expect to consider.

I ignited my **persistence** trait to turn a "no" into a "yes" when attempting to transfer law schools. Ignite your persistence trait whenever you are told "no" to something you are passionate about, such as getting your dream job, starting your dream business, or pursing your dream career. If you are truly passionate about something, never give up easily. Pursue it with persistence, and watch your desires come to life.

I ignited my **motivation** trait when I received my first job rejection letter. I could not convince that firm to hire me, but I had to remain motivated to gain employment elsewhere. Ignite your motivation trait regularly because it is like a daily vitamin. Sometimes when you are faced with disappointments and rejection, the other traits may not help you overcome the situation. For example, every job won't be the perfect fit for you, no matter how persistent you are, but you must remain motivated to find the job, career, or situation that is perfect for you.

I ignited my **self-worth/self-esteem** trait when I wasn't promoted fast enough in the "delay" season of my career. Ignite your self-worth/self-esteem trait whenever a situation leads you to self-doubt or self-pity or causes you to question your ability and self-worth. Remember, you are responsible for your own happiness and self-development. Never let what other people think of you or how they treat you determine how you value yourself. Read an empowering message or book or take a class to improve your gifts and talents. This will remind you of your self-worth and/or improve your skill set and, ultimately, your self-esteem. Never hesitate to improve your own self-esteem/self-worth.

I ignited my **faith** trait when I decided to quit my job and start my own law practice. Ignite your faith trait whenever you step into unchartered territory, such as starting a new business, relocating, receiving a poor medical prognosis, or even starting a new relationship. Sometimes you have to rely on a higher authority when the results you seek are unpredictable. You must activate your faith, and trust in God, Allah, Jehovah, or whatever higher power you believe in. Faith is essential to both life and success.

While on your life's journey and soaring beyond your adversities, you must ultimately step into your Purpose to be truly fulfilled. We are all given a Purpose, and your life experiences lead you to discover what your Purpose is. Your Purpose is your assignment. It's the reason you are here. Your Purpose is your voice to the world, your gift. I discovered that my Purpose is to inspire, motivate, and impact the lives of others both within and outside of the legal community. As I live in my Purpose, I share my story with the world and inspire others to soar beyond their adversities and live a purposeful life, too.

You will know when it's time to step into your Purpose because you will suddenly notice a void in your life needing to be filled. You will realize that you are not living a life of complete fulfillment. When you reach this point, reflect upon your experiences, and determine which life experiences bring you the most fulfillment, despite the many adversities you encountered along the way. Your Purpose is your passion and another person's inspiration. Recognize it, own it, and walk in it!

Thank you for sharing my journey with me and allowing me to share my story with you. Now that you are empowered by knowing the eight essential character traits you must ignite to soar beyond your heels of adversity and step into your Purpose, I hereby challenge you to take action—GO SOAR!

Acknowledgements

I would like to thank my parents, Naomi Rainey and Cleveland McPherson, Sr., for your unwavering love and support. My brother Cleveland McPherson, Jr., thank you for being not only a brother, but a confidant and friend. My sister Shakeerah T. McPherson, the boss lady of my life, thank you for your unconditional love, support, and continuous encouragement. A.J. Nolton, thanks for cheering me on and pushing me outside of my comfort zone. My brother David Whatley, thanks for becoming a part of my life, and I look forward to our growing relationship. My sister-cousin Francine Potts, thank you for your love and support.

A special thank you to some special

people who have contributed to the publication of this book: my insightful editor Cori Nicole Smith Wamsley to whom I am extremely grateful; my awesome photographer Ricki Cody; my super talented makeup artist Erica Nikole; and the amazing Kathy and Steve Kidd and the entire Kidd Marketing Team. Thank you all for your amazing contributions that have led to the success of this project.

www.ingramcontent.com/pod-product-compliance
Lightning Source LLC
Chambersburg PA
CBHW071814200526
45169CB00017B/241